PRESENTED TO

ON

BY

The
PRAYER
of JABEZ

Breaking Through to the Blessed Life

BRUCE WILKINSON

with DAVID KOPP

Illustrations by C. MICHAEL DUDASH

BLUE COTTAGE GIFTS™
a Division of Multnomah Publishers, Inc.

Multnomah® Publishers *Sisters, Oregon*

The Prayer of Jabez

Published by Multnomah Publishers, Inc.
© 2000 by Bruce Wilkinson
ISBN 1-57673-810-8 (Gift Book)
ISBN 1-57673-733-0 (Hardback)
ISBN 1-57673-857-4 (Leather)

Scipture quotations are from:
The Holy Bible, New King James Version © 1984 by Thomas Nelson, Inc.
Also quoted: *The Living Bible* (TLB) © 1971. Used by permission of
Tyndale House Publishers, Inc. All rights reserved.

Multnomah is a trademark of Multnomah Publishers, Inc. and is registered
in the U.S. Patent and Trademark Office.

The colophon is a trademark of Multnomah Publishers, Inc.
Printed in China

The paintings on pages 16–17, "If Two Shall Agree," and 74–75, "A Father's
Heritage," are the property of the MasterPeace® Collection, a division of
DaySpring® Cards, P.O. Box 1010, Siloam Springs, AR 72761.

Blue Cottage Gifts™ is a division of Multnomah Publishers, Inc.®

For information:
    Multnomah Publishers, Inc.
    PO Box 1720
    Sisters, Oregon 97759

01 02 03 04 05 06 — 10 9 8 7 6 5 4 3 2 1 0

Table of Contents

To all who—like those Christians in the book of Acts—

look at who they are now and who they'll never be,

and what they can do now and what they'll never

be able to do…and still ask God for the world.

Without the friendship, commitment, and skill of my writing

partner and editor David Kopp, the early help of my

previous editor Larry Libby, and the encouragement

of my publishing friend John Van Diest, the message

of this book would not have found its way to paper.

I am so thankful that the Lord brought us together.

Preface

Dear Reader,

I want to teach you how to pray a daring prayer that God always answers.
It is brief—only one sentence with four parts—and tucked away in the Bible,
but I believe it contains the key to a life of extraordinary favor with God.

This petition has radically changed what I expect from God and what
I experience every day by His power. In fact, thousands of believers who are
applying its truths are seeing miracles happen on a regular basis.

Will you join me for a personal exploration of Jabez?

I hope you will!

Bruce Wilkinson

LITTLE PRAYER, GIANT PRIZE

Jabez called on the God of Israel

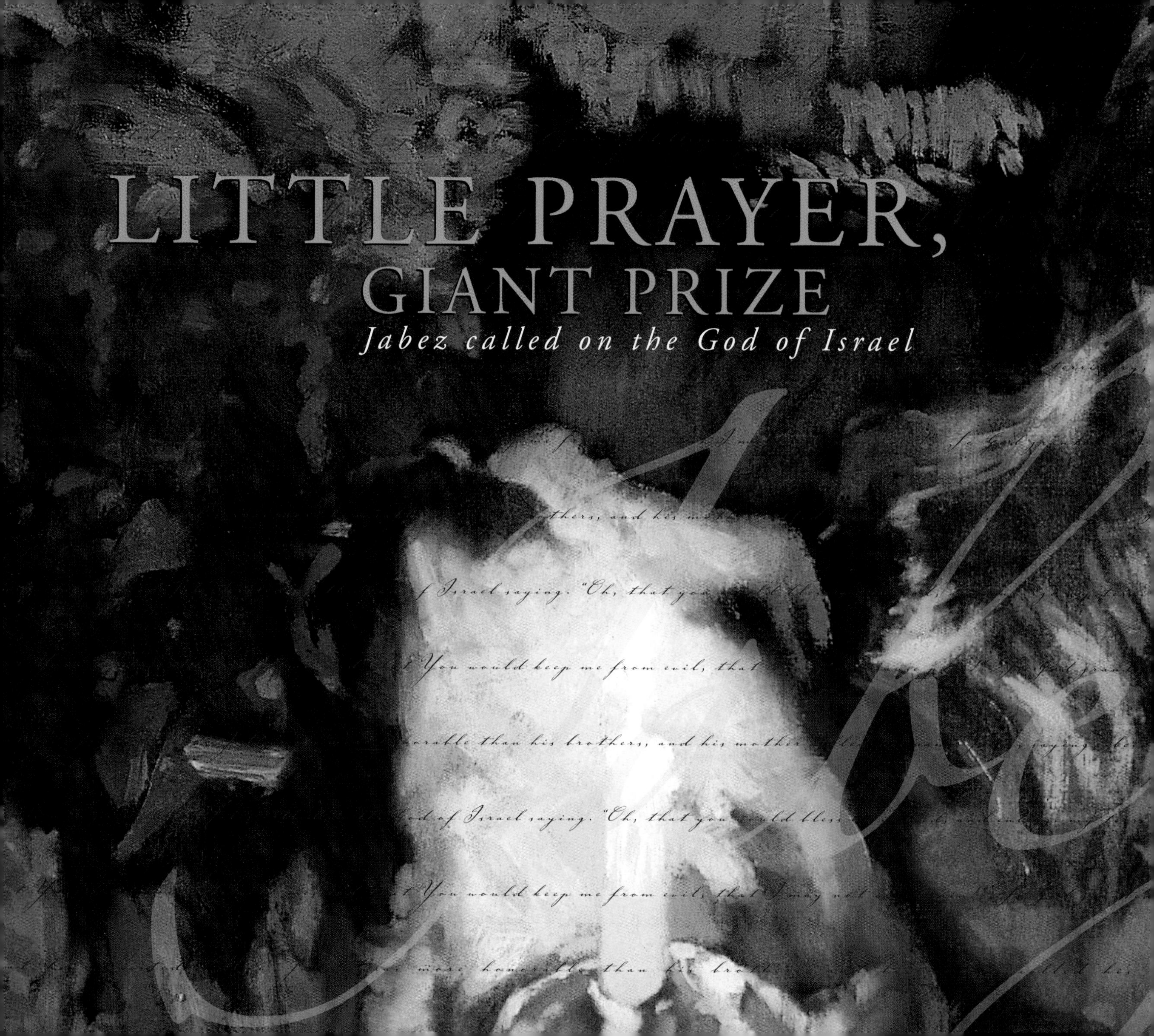

The little book you're holding is about what happens when ordinary Christians decide to reach for an extraordinary life—which, as it turns out, is exactly the kind God promises.

My own story starts in a kitchen with yellow counters and Texas-sized raindrops pelting the window. It was my senior year of seminary in Dallas. Darlene, my wife, and I were finding ourselves spending more and more time thinking and praying about what would come next. Where should I throw my energy, passion, and training? What did God want for us as a couple? I stood in our kitchen thinking again about a challenge I'd heard from the seminary chaplain, Dr. Richard Seume. "Want a bigger vision for your life?" he had asked earlier that week. "Sign up to be a gimper for God."

A gimper, as Seume explained it, was someone who always does a little more than what's required or expected. In the furniture business, for example, gimping is putting the finishing touches on the upholstery, patiently applying the ornamental extras that are a mark of quality and value.

Dr. Seume took as his text the briefest of Bible biographies: "Now Jabez was more honorable than his brothers" (1 CHRONICLES 4:9). Jabez wanted to be more and do more for God, and— as we discover by the end of verse 10—God granted him his request.

End of verse. End of Bible story.

Lord, I think I want to be a gimper for You, I prayed as I looked out the window at the blustery spring rain. But I was puzzled. *What exactly did Jabez do to rise above the rest? Why did God answer his prayer?* I wondered. For that matter, why did God even include Jabez's miniprofile in the Bible?

Maybe it was the raindrops running down the windowpanes. Suddenly my thoughts ran past verse 9.

I picked up my Bible and read verse 10—the prayer of Jabez. Something in his prayer would explain the mystery. It had to. Pulling a chair up to the yellow counter, I bent over my Bible, and reading the prayer over and over, I searched with all my heart for the future God had for someone as ordinary as I.

The next morning, I prayed Jabez's prayer word for word.

And the next.

And the next.

Thirty years later, I haven't stopped.

If you were to ask me what sentence—other than my prayer for salvation—has revolutionized my life and ministry the most, I would tell you that it was the cry of a gimper named Jabez, who is still remembered not for what he did, but for what he prayed—and for what happened next.

In the pages of this little book, I want to introduce you to the amazing truths in Jabez's prayer for blessing and prepare you to expect God's astounding answers to it *as a regular part of your life experience.*

How do I know that it will significantly impact you? Because of my experience and the testimony of hundreds of others around the world with whom I've shared these principles. Because, even more importantly, the Jabez prayer distills God's powerful will for your future. Finally, because it reveals that your Father longs to give you so much more than you may have ever thought to ask for.

Just ask the man who had no future.

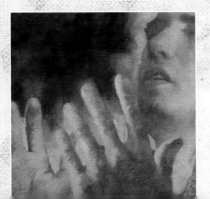

prodigy
GENEALOGY
THE PRODIGY OF THE GENEALOGY

Someone once said there is really very little difference between people—but that little difference makes a great deal of difference. Jabez doesn't stand astride the Old Testament like a Moses or a David or light up the book of Acts like those early Christians who turned the world upside down. But one thing is sure: The little difference in his life made all the difference.

You could think of him as the Prodigy of the Genealogy, or maybe the Bible's Little Big Man. You'll find him hiding in the least-read section of one of the least-read books of the Bible.

The first nine chapters of 1 Chronicles are taken up with the official family tree of the Hebrew tribes, beginning with Adam and proceeding through thousands of years to Israel's return from captivity. Talk about boring! The long lists of unfamiliar and difficult names—more than five hundred of them—are likely to make even the bravest Bible student turn back.

Take chapter 4. *The descendants of Judah: Perez, Hezron, and Carmi, and Hur, and Shobal....* And that's just the beginning.

> *Ahumai*
>
> *Ishma*
>
> *Idbash*
>
> *Hazelelponi*
>
> *Anub...*

I'd forgive you if you suddenly considered putting this little book aside and reaching for your TV remote. But stay with me. Because forty-four names into the chapter, a story suddenly breaks through:

> Now Jabez was more honorable than his brothers, and his mother called his name Jabez, saying, "Because I bore him in pain." And Jabez called on the God of Israel saying, "Oh, that You would bless me indeed, and enlarge my territory, that Your hand would be with me, and that You would keep me from evil, that I may not cause pain!" So God granted him what he requested. (1 CHRONICLES 4:9–10)

In the next verse, the roll call for the tribe of Judah picks up as if nothing has happened— *Chelub, Shuah, Mehir....*

Something about this man Jabez had caused the historian to pause in middrone, clear his throat, and switch tactics. "Ah, wait a minute!" he seems to interject. "You just *gotta* know something about this guy named Jabez. He stands head and shoulders above the rest!"

difference

the little difference made all the difference

What was the secret to the enduring reputation of Jabez? You can search from front to back in your Bible, as I have, and you won't find any more information than we have in these two brief verses:

- Things started badly for a person no one had ever heard of.

- He prayed an unusual, one-sentence prayer.

- Things ended extraordinarily well.

Clearly, the outcome can be traced to his prayer. Something about Jabez's simple, direct request to God changed his life and left a permanent mark on the history books of Israel:

> Oh, that You would bless me indeed,
> and enlarge my territory,
> that Your hand would be with me,
> and that You would keep me from evil.

At first glance, the four requests may strike you as sincere, sensible, even noble, but not terribly remarkable. Yet just under the surface of each lies a giant paradigm breaker that runs exactly opposite to the way you and I usually think. In the pages to come, I want to show you just how dramatically each of Jabez's requests can release something miraculous in your life.

beyond LIMITS

LIVING BEYOND THE LIMITS

When was the last time God worked through you in such a way that you knew beyond doubt that God had done it? In fact, when was the last time you saw miracles happen on a regular basis in *your* life? If you're like most believers I've met, you wouldn't know how to ask for that kind of experience, or even if you should.

What I have to share with you has been opening up lives to God's mighty working for many years. Recently, I was in Dallas to teach on the Jabez blessing to an audience of 9,000. Later over lunch, a man said to me, "Bruce, I heard you preach the message of Jabez fifteen years ago, and I haven't stopped praying it. The change has been so overwhelming I have just never stopped."

Across the table, another friend agreed. He said he'd been praying Jabez's little prayer for ten years with similar results. The man next to him, a heart surgeon from Indianapolis, said he had been praying it for five.

I told them, "Friends, I've been praying Jabez for more than *half my life!*"

Because you're reading this book, I believe you share my desire to reach for a life that will be "more honorable" for God. Not that you wish others to reach for less, but for you, nothing but God's fullest blessing will do. When you stand before Him to give your accounting, your deepest longing is to hear, "Well done!"

God really does have unclaimed blessings waiting for you, my friend. I know it sounds impossible—even embarrassingly suspicious in our self-serving day. Yet that very exchange—your want for God's plenty—has been His loving will for your life from eternity past. And with a handful of core commitments on your part, you can proceed from this day forward with the confidence and expectation that your heavenly Father will bring it to pass for you.

ask for a miracle

Think of it this way: Instead of standing near the river's edge, asking for a cup of water to get you through each day, you'll do something unthinkable—you will take the little prayer with the giant prize and *jump into the river!* At that moment, you will begin to let the loving currents of God's grace and power carry you along. God's great plan for you will surround you and sweep you forward into the profoundly important and satisfying life He has waiting.

If that is what you want, keep reading.

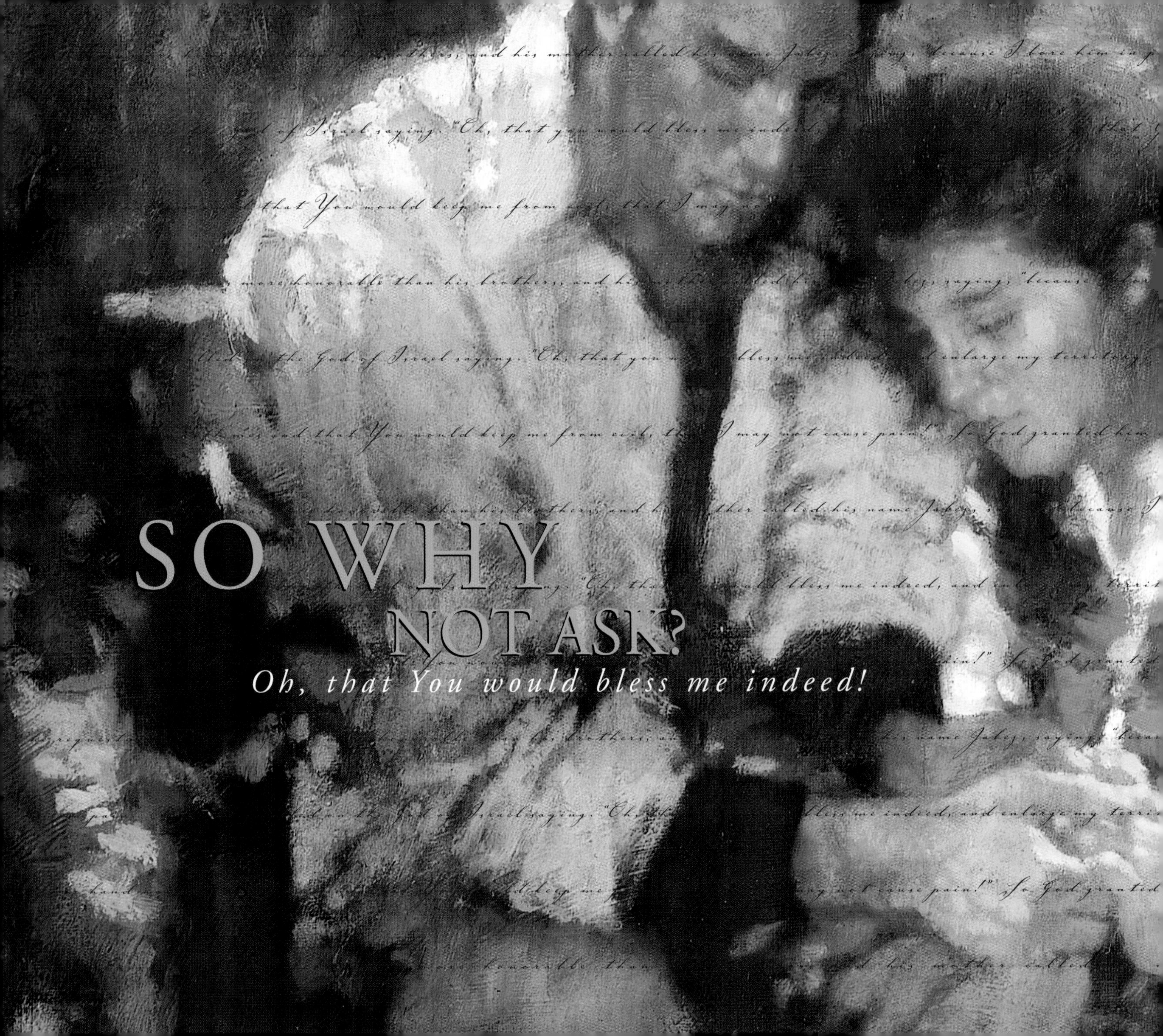

SO WHY NOT ASK?

Oh, that You would bless me indeed!

You're at a spiritual retreat in the mountains with others who want to experience a fuller Christian life. For the duration of the retreat everyone has been matched with a mentor. Yours is in his seventies, and he's been touching lives for God longer than you've been alive.

On the way to the showers the first morning, you walk past his room. His door is ajar, and he has just knelt down to pray. You can't resist. *How exactly does a giant of the faith begin his prayers?* you wonder.

You pause and lean closer. Will he pray for revival? Pray for the hungry around the world? Pray for you?

But this is what you hear: "O Lord, I beg you first and most this morning, please bless…*me!*"

Startled at such a selfish prayer, you pad down the hall to your shower. But as you're adjusting the water temperature, a thought hits you. It's so obvious, you can't believe you haven't thought it before:

Great men of the faith think differently than the rest of us.

By the time you're dressed and heading for breakfast, you're sure of it. The reason some men and women of faith rise above the rest, you decide, is that they think and pray differently than those around them.

Is it possible that God wants you to be "selfish" in your prayers? To ask for more—and more again—from your Lord? I've met so many earnest Christians who take it as a sign of immaturity to think such thoughts. They assume they'll seem impolite or greedy if they ask God for too many blessings.

Maybe you think like that. If you do, I want to show you that such a prayer is not the self-centered act it might appear, but a supremely spiritual one and exactly the kind of request our Father longs to hear.

First, let's take a closer look at Jabez's story.

Great men of the faith think differently

BUT GAIN

NOT PAIN, BUT GAIN

As far as we can tell, Jabez lived in southern Israel after the conquest of Canaan and during the time of the judges. He was born into the tribe of Judah and eventually became the notable head of a clan. Yet his story really begins with his name: "His mother called his name Jabez, saying, 'Because I bore him in pain.'"

In Hebrew, the word *Jabez* means "pain." A literal rendering could read, "He causes [or will cause] pain."

Doesn't sound like the start of a promising life, does it?

All babies arrive with a certain amount of pain, but something about Jabez's birth went beyond the usual—so much so that his mother chose to memorialize it in her son's name. Why? The pregnancy or the delivery may have been traumatic. Perhaps the baby was born breech. Or perhaps the mother's pain was emotional—maybe the child's father abandoned her during the pregnancy; maybe he had died; maybe the family had fallen into such financial straits that the prospect of another mouth to feed brought only fear and worry.

than the rest of us.

Only God knows for sure what caused the pain of this anguished mother. Not that it made much difference to young Jabez. He grew up with a name any boy would love to hate. Imagine if you had to go through childhood enduring the teasing of bullies, the daily reminders of your unwelcome arrival, and mocking questions like, "So, young man, what was your mother thinking?"

Yet by far the heaviest burden of Jabez's name was how it defined his future. In Bible times, a man and his name were so intimately related that "to cut off the name" of an individual amounted to the same thing as killing him. A name was often taken as a wish for or prophecy about the child's future. For example, Jacob can mean "grabber," a good one-word biography for that scheming patriarch. Naomi and her husband named their two sons Mahlon and Chilion. Translation? "Puny" and "pining." And that was exactly what they were. Both of them died in early adulthood. Solomon means "peace," and sure enough, he became the first king of Israel to reign without going to war. A name that meant "pain" didn't bode well for Jabez's future.

bless me . . .

Despite his dismal prospects, Jabez found a way out. He had grown up hearing about the God of Israel who had freed his forefathers from slavery, rescued them from powerful enemies, and established them in a land of plenty. By the time he was an adult, Jabez believed and fervently hoped in this God of miracles and new beginnings.

So why not ask for one?

That's what he did. He prayed the biggest, most improbable request imaginable:

"Oh, that You would bless me *indeed…!*"

I love the urgency, the personal vulnerability of his plea. In Hebrew, adding "indeed" to this prayer was like adding five exclamation points, or writing the request in capital letters and underlining it.

In my mind's eye, I picture Jabez standing before a massive gate recessed into a sky-high wall. Weighed down by the sorrow of his past and the dreariness of his present, he sees before him only impossibility—a future shut off. But raising his hands to heaven, he cries out, "Father, oh, Father! Please bless me! And what I really mean is…bless me a lot!"

With the last word, the transformation begins. He hears a tremendous crack. Then a groan. Then a rumble as the huge gate swings away from him in a wide arc. There, stretching to the horizon, are fields of blessings.

And Jabez steps forward into another life.

indeed!

NOT ABOUT SNEEZING

BLESSING IS NOT ABOUT SNEEZING

Before we can ask for God's blessing with confidence, we need a clear understanding of what the word means. We hear "bless" or "blessing" intoned from every pulpit. We ask God to bless the missionaries, the kids, and the food we're about to eat. It's something Grandma says when she hears you sneeze.

No wonder the meaning of blessing gets watered down to something vague and innocuous like "Have a nice day." No wonder so many Christians aren't as desperate as Jabez was to receive it!

To bless in the biblical sense means to ask for or to impart supernatural favor. When we ask for God's blessing, we're not asking for more of what we could get for ourselves. We're crying out for the wonderful, unlimited goodness that only God has the power to know about or give to us. This kind of richness is what the writer was referring to in Proverbs: "The Lord's blessing is our greatest wealth; all our work adds nothing to it" (PROVERBS 10:22, TLB).

Notice a radical aspect of Jabez's request for blessing: *He left it entirely up to God to decide what the blessings would be and where, when, and how Jabez would receive them.* This kind of radical trust in God's good intentions toward us has nothing in common with the popular gospel that you should ask God for a Cadillac, a six-figure income, or some other material sign that you have found a way to cash in on your connection with Him. Instead, the Jabez blessing focuses like a laser on our wanting for ourselves nothing more and nothing less than what God wants for us.

When we seek God's blessing as the ultimate value in life, we are throwing ourselves entirely into the river of His will and power and purposes for us. All our other needs become secondary to what we really want—which is to become wholly immersed in what God is trying to do in us, through us, and around us for His glory.

Let me tell you a guaranteed by-product of sincerely seeking His blessing: Your life will become marked by miracles. How do I know? Because He promises it, and I've seen it happen in my own! God's power to accomplish great things suddenly finds no obstruction in you. You're moving in His direction. You're praying for exactly what God desires. Suddenly the unhindered forces of heaven can begin to accomplish God's perfect will—through you. And you will be the first to notice!

But there's a catch.

MR. JONES GOES TO HEAVEN

What if you found out that God had it in mind to send you twenty-three specific blessings today, but you got only one? What do you suppose the reason would be?

There's a little fable about a Mr. Jones who dies and goes to heaven. Peter is waiting at the gates to give him a tour. Amid the splendor of golden streets, beautiful mansions, and choirs of angels that Peter shows him, Mr. Jones notices an odd-looking building. He thinks it looks like an enormous warehouse—it has no windows and only one door. But when he asks to see inside, Peter hesitates. "You really don't want to see what's in there," he tells the new arrival.

Why would there be any secrets in heaven? Jones wonders. *What incredible surprise could be waiting for me in there?* When the official tour is over he's still wondering, so he asks again to see inside the structure.

Finally Peter relents. When the apostle opens the door, Mr. Jones almost knocks him over in his haste to enter. It turns out that the enormous building is filled with row after row of shelves, floor to ceiling, each stacked neatly with white boxes tied in red ribbons.

"These boxes all have names on them," Mr. Jones muses aloud. Then turning to Peter he asks, "Do I have one?"

"Yes, you do." Peter tries to guide Mr. Jones back outside. "Frankly," Peter says, "if I were you…." But Mr. Jones is already dashing toward the "J" aisle to find his box.

Peter follows, shaking his head. He catches up with Mr. Jones just as he is slipping the red ribbon off his box and popping the lid. Looking inside, Jones has a moment of instant recognition, and he lets out a deep sigh like the ones Peter has heard so many times before.

Because there in Mr. Jones's white box are all the blessings that God wanted to give to him while he was on earth…but Mr. Jones had never asked.

"Ask," promised Jesus, "and it will be given to you" (MATTHEW 7:7). "You do not have because you do not ask," said James (JAMES 4:2). Even though there is no limit to God's goodness, if you didn't ask Him for a blessing yesterday, you didn't get all that you were supposed to have.

That's the catch—if you don't ask for His blessing, you forfeit those that come to you only when you ask. In the same way that a father is honored to have a child beg for his blessing, your Father is delighted to respond generously when His blessing is what you covet most.

nature
IS TO BLESS

GOD'S NATURE IS TO BLESS

Perhaps you think that your name is just another word for pain or trouble, or that the legacy you have been handed from your family circumstances is nothing but a liability. You just don't feel like a candidate for blessing.

Or perhaps you're one of those Christians who thinks that once you're saved, God's blessings sort of drizzle over your life at a predetermined rate, no matter what you do. No extra effort required.

Or perhaps you have slipped into a ledger-keeping mindset with God. In your blessings account you have a column for deposits and one for withdrawals. Has God been unusually kind to you lately? Then you think that you shouldn't expect, much less ask for, Him to credit your account. You might even think He should ignore you for a while, or even debit your account by sending some trouble your way.

This kind of thinking is a sin and a trap! When Moses said to God on Mount Sinai, "Show me Your glory" (EXODUS 33:18), he was asking for a more intimate understanding of God. In response, God described Himself as "the Lord, the Lord God, merciful and gracious, longsuffering, and abounding in goodness and truth" (34:6).

a simple prayer

Incredible! The very nature of God is to have goodness in so much abundance that it overflows into our unworthy lives. If you think about God in any other way than that, I'm asking you to change the way you think. Why not make it a lifelong commitment to ask God every day to bless you—and while He's at it, bless you *a lot?*

God's bounty is limited only by us, not by His resources, power, or willingness to give. Jabez was blessed simply because he refused to let any obstacle, person, or opinion loom larger than God's nature. And God's nature is to bless.

His kindness in recording Jabez's story in the Bible is proof that it's not who you are, or what your parents decided for you, or what you were "fated" to be that counts. What counts is knowing who you want to be and asking for it.

Through a simple, believing prayer, you can change your future. You can change what happens one minute from now.

LIVING LARGE
FOR GOD
Oh, that You would enlarge my territory!

The next part of the Jabez prayer—a plea for more territory—is where you ask God to enlarge your life so you can make a greater impact for Him.

From both the context and the results of Jabez's prayer, we can see that there was more to his request than a simple desire for more real estate. He wanted more influence, more responsibility, and more opportunity *to make a mark for the God of Israel.*

Depending on the version you're reading, the word *territory* can also be translated coast or borders. For Jabez and his contemporaries, that word carried the same emotional power as the words *homestead* or *frontier* did for generations of American pioneers. It spoke of a place of one's own with plenty of room to grow.

enlarge my territory!

In Jabez's time part of Israel's recent national history was Joshua's conquest of Canaan and the partitioning of the Promised Land into chunks of real estate for each tribe. When Jabez cried out to God, "Enlarge my territory!" he was looking at his present circumstances and concluding, "Surely I was born for more than this!" As a farmer or herdsman, he looked over the spread his family had passed down to him, ran his eye down the fence lines, visited the boundary markers, calculated the potential—and made a decision: *Everything you've put under my care, O Lord—take it, and enlarge it.*

If Jabez had worked on Wall Street, he might have prayed, "Lord, increase the value of my investment portfolios." When I talk to presidents of companies, I often talk to them about this particular mind-set. When Christian executives ask me, "Is it right for me to ask God for more business?" my response is, "Absolutely!" If you're doing your business God's way, it's not only right to ask for more, but He is waiting for you to ask. Your business is the territory God has entrusted to you. He wants you to accept it as a significant opportunity to touch individual lives, the business community, and the larger world for His glory. Asking Him to enlarge that opportunity brings Him only delight.

Suppose Jabez had been a wife and a mother. Then the prayer might have gone: "Lord, add to my family, favor my key relationships, multiply for Your glory the influence of my household." Your home is the single most powerful arena on earth to change a life for God. Why wouldn't He want you to be mighty for Him?

No matter what your vocation, the highest form of Jabez's prayer for more territory might sound something like:

> *O God and King, please expand my opportunities*
> *and my impact in such a way that I touch more lives*
> *for Your glory. Let me do more for You!*

When you pray like this, things get pretty exciting.

moving BOUNDARIES

MOVING THE BOUNDARY LINES

During a weeklong speaking engagement some years ago at a large Christian college in California, I challenged students to pray the Jabez prayer for more blessing and greater influence. I suggested that the 2000-member student body set a ministry goal worthy of a college of its stature.

"Why not look at the globe and pick an island," I suggested. "When you have it picked out, put together a team of students, charter an airliner, then take over the island for God."

Some students roared. Some questioned my sanity. But nearly everyone listened. I persisted. I had been to the island of Trinidad and seen the need, I told them. "You should ask God for Trinidad," I said. "And a DC-10."

I had no immediate takers.

Still, the challenge prompted a flurry of stimulating conversations. I found most students eager to do something meaningful with their time and talents, but unsure where to start. They usually made a point of listing their deficiencies in skill, money, courage, or opportunity.

I spent much of that week asking a question: If the God of heaven loves you infinitely and wants you in His presence every moment, and if He knows that heaven is a much better place for you, then why on earth has He left you here? With student after student, I pressed home what I understand to be a biblical answer to that question: because God wants you to be moving out your boundary lines, taking in new territory for Him—maybe an island—and reaching people in His name.

God was at work. A week after I had returned home, I received a letter from a student named Warren. He told me that he and his friend Dave had decided to challenge God's power and ask Him to bless them and enlarge their borders. Specifically, they had prayed that God would give them the opportunity to witness to the governor of the state *that weekend*. Throwing their sleeping bags in Warren's '63 Plymouth Valiant, they had driven the 400 miles to the capital to pound on doors.

The letter continued:

> By Sunday night when we got back from Sacramento, this is what had happened:
>
> We had expressed our faith to two gas station attendants, four security guards, the head of the U.S. National Guard, the director of the Department of Health, Education, and Welfare for the state of California, the head of the California Highway Patrol, the governor's secretary, and finally the governor himself.
>
> As God is making us grow, we are thankful and scared stiff. Thanks again for your challenge!

That was just the beginning. Over the next weeks and months, a vision for more territory swept the campus. By fall, a student team headed by Warren and Dave had mounted a major mission project for the following summer. They called it Operation Jabez. Their objective: assemble a team of self-supported student workers, charter a jet, and—you guessed it—fly to the island of Trinidad for a summer of ministry.

And that is exactly what they did. One hundred and twenty-six students and faculty signed up. By the time the jet took off fully loaded from Los Angeles, Operation Jabez boasted trained teams ready to minister through drama, construction, vacation Bible school, music, and home visitation. The college president called Operation Jabez the single most significant student ministry venture in the college's history.

Two students had asked God to enlarge their territory—and He did! One little prayer had remapped boundary lines and impacted the lives of thousands of people.

my APPOINTMENT

"I THINK THIS IS MY APPOINTMENT"

The Jabez prayer is a revolutionary request. Just as it is highly unusual to hear anyone pray, "God, please bless me!" so it is rare to hear anyone plead, "God, please give me more ministry!" Most of us think our lives are too full already. But when, in faith, you start to pray for more ministry, amazing things occur. As your opportunities expand, your ability and resources supernaturally increase, too. Right away you'll sense the pleasure God feels in your request and His urgency to accomplish great things through you.

People will show up on your doorstep or at the table next to you. They'll start saying things that surprise even them. They'll ask for something—they're not sure what—and wait for your reply.

I call these encounters Jabez appointments.

I remember the first time I asked for one. It was in a very surprising place—aboard a ship off the coast of Turkey. I was traveling alone, scouting a tour company that specialized in taking groups around the Mediterranean, following in the footsteps of the early church. We had enjoyed beautiful days aboard with plenty of time for me to work on various projects, but I was getting lonelier by the day. The morning we anchored at Patmos, the island where John wrote the book of Revelation, I hit bottom.

Instead of taking the guided tour, I walked around the streets of the little port talking to the Lord. *Lord, I feel so homesick and weak,* I prayed. *But I want to be Your servant. Even now, enlarge my borders. Send somebody who needs me.*

Entering a small square, I took a table at an outdoor café and ordered a cup of coffee. A few minutes later I heard a man's voice behind me. "You on the cruise ship?"

I looked up to see a young man walking toward me. "Yes, I am," I said.
"How about you?"

He said he was an American living on the island, then asked if he could join me. His name was Terry. Within minutes he was pouring out his story. As it turned out, his marriage was on the rocks. In fact, that day was the end. His wife had said she would be gone by evening.

You know what I was thinking by that time, don't you? Okay, Lord. I think this is my appointment. And I accept....

"Do you want your wife to leave?" I asked. He said no.

"Open to a couple of ideas?" I offered. When he said yes, I knew it was the Lord's confirmation of another Jabez experience. I spent the next hour talking through several key biblical principles for a happy marriage. Terry hadn't heard of even one before.

By the time I was done, Terry was so anxious to give his new insights a chance to save his marriage that he jumped to his feet. "Listen, Terry," I said, "I really want to hear how things go for you and your wife today. Whatever happens, come by the boat before we sail and tell me, okay?"

Terry agreed, waved, and was gone. By that evening, everyone was back on board. I walked the deck, waiting. I was still lonely, kind of frustrated, and starting to second-guess what had gone on inside Terry over coffee. When the captain ordered the final blast announcing our departure, I walked to the back of the ship where the crew was busy throwing off the stern lines. And there, running toward us along the shore, came a young couple hand in hand. When they got close enough to see me hanging over the rail, they started yelling. "It worked! It worked! We're together!"

The rest of the voyage I was so exhilarated at what God had done that I felt like I was floating without help from the ship. God had made an appointment for that young man and me. And He had been bringing us toward each other from the moment I had asked for a larger life in His service.

living GOD'S MATH

LIVING BY GOD'S MATH

Whatever our gifts, education, or vocation might be, our calling is to do God's work on earth. If you want, you can call it living out your faith for others. You can call it ministry. You can call it every Christian's day job. But whatever you call it, God is looking for people who want to do more of it, because sadly, most believers seem to shrink from living at this level of blessing and influence.

For most of us, our reluctance comes from getting our numbers right, but our arithmetic completely wrong. For example, when we're deciding what size territory God has in mind for us, we keep an equation in our heart that adds up something like this:

> My abilities
> + Experience
> + Training
> + My personality and appearance
> + My past
> + The expectations of others
> _____
> = My assigned territory.

not by might

No matter how many sermons we've heard about God's power to work through us, we simply gloss over the meaning of that one little word *through*. Sure, we say we want God to work through us, but what we really mean is *by* or *in association with*. Yet God's reminder to us is the same one He gave the Jews when they returned from captivity to a decimated homeland: "Not by might nor by power but by My Spirit, says the LORD of hosts" (ZECHARIAH 4:6).

Our God specializes in working through normal people who believe in a supernormal God who will do His work through them. What He's waiting for is the invitation. That means God's math would look more like this:

> My willingness and weakness
> + God's will and supernatural power
> = My expanding territory.

When you start asking in earnest—begging—for more influence and responsibility with which to honor Him, God will bring opportunities and people into your path. You can trust Him that He will never send someone to you whom you cannot help by His leading and strength. You'll nearly always feel fear when you begin to take new territory for Him, but you'll also experience the tremendous thrill of God carrying you along as you're doing it. You'll be like John and Peter, who were given the words to say at the moment they needed them.

nor by power
but by my spirit

One day in answer to Darlene's prayers for an enlarged ministry, a neighbor we hardly knew came knocking at our door. "Ma'am," she said through tears, "my husband is dying, and I have nobody to talk to. Can you help me?"

Larger borders. An appointment to keep.

Recently on a cross-country train trip, I prayed again that God would enlarge my borders. While I was eating in the dining car, I asked the Lord to send someone who needed Him. A woman sat down across the table from me and said she needed to ask me a question. She knew my name, but little else about me. She looked deeply agitated.

"What can I do for you?" I asked.

"I'm afraid of the Antichrist," she replied. "For fifty years, I've lived in dread that I won't recognize him when he comes and that I'll be deceived by him and receive the mark of the beast."

That point-blank question from a woman I'll never meet again led to a moving conversation and a beautiful spiritual deliverance.

Larger borders. An appointment to keep.

front
ROW SEAT

YOUR FRONT-ROW SEAT

To pray for larger borders is to ask for a miracle—it's that simple. A miracle is an intervention by God to make something happen that wouldn't normally happen. That, and nothing less, was what Jabez had to have to transcend his name and transform his circumstances.

Do you believe miracles still happen? Many Christians I've met do not. I remind them that miracles don't have to break natural law to be a supernatural event. When Christ stilled the storm, He didn't set aside universal law—the storm would eventually have subsided on its own. Instead, He directed the weather pattern. When Elijah prayed for it to stop raining, God directed the natural cycle of drought and rain.

In the same way, God's miracle-working powers were clearly in evidence when, knowing Terry's need, He brought us together on Patmos. And when, knowing the needs of the woman on the train, He arranged a conversation between us.

The most exhilarating miracles in my life have always started with a bold request to expand God's kingdom *a lot.* When you take little steps, you don't need God. It's when you thrust yourself in the mainstream of God's plans for this world—which are beyond our ability to accomplish—and plead with Him, *Lord, use me—give me more ministry for You!*—that you release miracles. At that moment, heaven sends angels, resources, strength, and the people you need. I've seen it happen hundreds of times.

God always intervenes when you put His agenda before yours and go for it! Amazingly, if you have prayed to the Lord to expand a border, you will recognize His divine answer. You'll have a front-row seat in a life of miracles.

for You

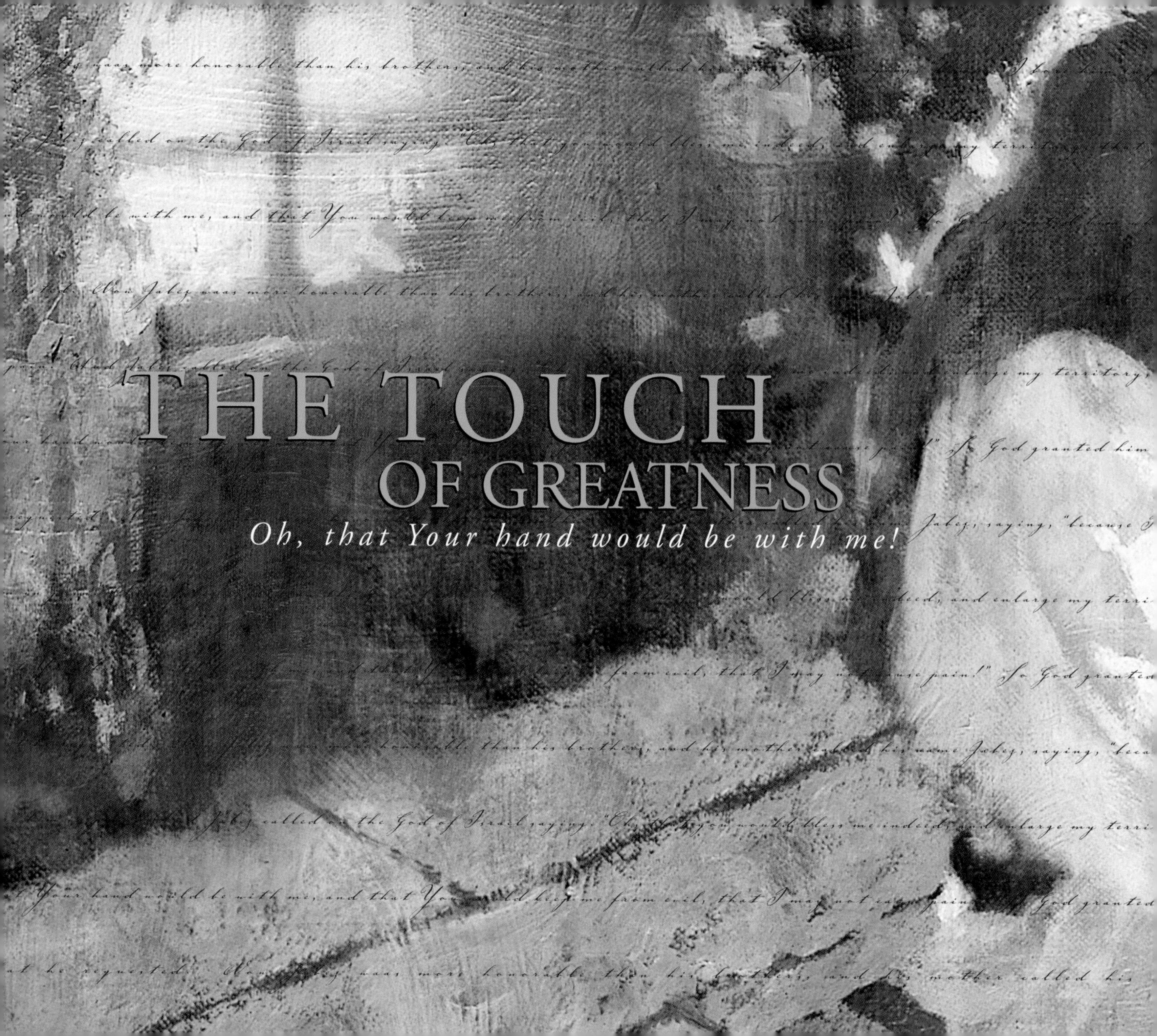

THE TOUCH OF GREATNESS

Oh, that Your hand would be with me!

Now you've done it. Gone over the edge. Gotten in too deep. Come up smack against the cold stone of reality. You are unable to hold on to the life you reached for….

Having dared to ask for an enlarged ministry, more than a few Christians have faltered at this point in their spiritual transformation. They've received blessings on a scale they hadn't imagined possible. They've seen God stretch the limits of their influence and opportunities.

But suddenly the rush of wind under their wings stops. Helpless, they start to plummet.

Sound familiar? Maybe your new business opportunities threaten to outrun your experience and resources. Maybe the teenagers who have started congregating in your kitchen suddenly seem to be influencing your family more negatively than you are influencing them positively. Maybe the new ministry opportunities you prayed for and received are turning out to require a person with much more ability than you will ever have.

You have taken up an armload of God's blessings, marched into new territory…and stumbled into overwhelming circumstances. When believers find themselves in this kind of unexpected quandary, they often feel afraid. Misled. Abandoned. A little angry.

I did….

Oh, that Your hand would be with me.

descending TO POWER

Talk about plummeting! I felt out of control and weak—nothing like a leader is supposed to feel—and most days all I could see was the ground rushing up at me. It was early in my ministry adventure, after doors had started to burst open on exciting new possibilities at Walk Thru the Bible. But I just couldn't shake the feeling that I was the wrong man for the job.

Extremely upset, I decided to seek the counsel of a trusted older man. John Mitchell was in his eighties then—a Yorkshire-born Bible teacher who had been a spiritual father to thousands. I told him what I thought God was calling me to do and then confessed my problem. I was still trying to describe my crisis in some detail when he broke in.

"Son," he said, in his kindly brogue, "that feeling you are running from is called dependence. It means you're walking with the Lord Jesus." He paused to let me take in his words, then continued. "Actually, the second you're not feeling dependent is the second you've backed away from truly living by faith."

I didn't like what I heard. "You're saying, Dr. Mitchell, that feeling that I just can't do it is what I'm supposed to be feeling?"

"Why certainly, young man!" he said, beaming. "That's the one all right."

It's a frightening and utterly exhilarating truth, isn't it? As God's chosen, blessed sons and daughters, we are expected to attempt something large enough that failure is guaranteed…unless God steps in. Take a minute to prayerfully try to comprehend how contrary that truth is to everything you would humanly choose:

• It goes against common sense.

• It contradicts your previous life experience.

• It seems to disregard your feelings, training, and need for security.

• It sets you up to look like a fool and a loser.

Yet it is God's plan for His most-honored servants.

I'll admit, big-screen heroes don't seem to put any stock in dependence—but you and I were made for it. Dependence upon God makes heroes of ordinary people like Jabez and you and me. How? We're forced to cry out with Jabez's third desperate plea:

"Oh, that Your hand would be with me!"

With that, we release God's power to accomplish His will and bring Him glory through all those seeming impossibilities.

Notice that Jabez did not begin his prayer by asking for God's hand to be with him. At that point, he didn't sense the need. Things were still manageable. His risks, and the fears that go with them, were minimal. But when his boundaries got moved out, and the kingdom-sized tasks of God's agenda started coming at him, Jabez knew he needed a divine hand—and fast. He could have turned back, or he could have tried to keep going in his own strength. Instead, he prayed.

If seeking God's blessings is our ultimate act of worship, and asking to do more for Him is our utmost ambition, then asking for God's hand upon us is our strategic choice to sustain and continue the great things that God has begun in our lives.

That's why you could call God's hand on you "the touch of greatness." You do not become great; you become dependent on the strong hand of God. Your surrendered need turns into His unlimited opportunity. And He becomes great through you.

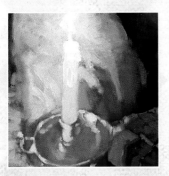

ladder
TO THE CLOUDS

A LADDER TO THE CLOUDS

One day when our kids were preschoolers, Darlene and I found ourselves with them at a large city park in southern California. It was the kind of park that makes a grown man wish he were a kid again. It had swings, monkey bars, and seesaws, but what was most enticing were the slides—not just one slide, but three—from small, to medium, to enormous. David, who was five at the time, took off like a shot for the small slide.

"Why don't you go down with him?" Darlene suggested.

But I had another idea. "Let's wait and see what happens," I said. So we relaxed on a nearby bench and watched. David clambered happily to the top of the smallest slide. He waved over at us with a big smile, then whizzed down.

Without hesitation he moved over to the medium-sized slide. He had climbed halfway up the ladder when he turned and looked at me. I looked away. He pondered his options for a moment, then carefully backed down one step at a time.

"Honey, you ought to go help him out," my wife said.

"Not yet," I replied, hoping the twinkle in my eye would reassure her that I wasn't just being careless.

David spent a few minutes at the bottom of the middle slide watching other kids climb up, whiz down, and run around to do it again. Finally his little mind was made up. He could do it. He climbed up…and slid down. Three times, in fact, without even looking at us.

Then we watched him turn and head toward the highest slide. Now Darlene was getting anxious. "Bruce, I don't think he should do that by himself. Do you?"

"No," I replied as calmly as possible. "But I don't think he will. Let's see what he does."

When David reached the bottom of the giant slide, he turned and called out, "Daddy!" But I glanced away again, pretending I couldn't hear him.

He peered up the ladder. In his young imagination, it must have reached to the clouds. He watched a teenage boy go hurtling down the slide. Then, against all odds, he decided to try. Step-by-step, hand over hand, he inched up the ladder. He hadn't reached a third of the way when he froze. By this time, the teenager was coming up behind him and yelled at him to get going. But David couldn't. He couldn't go up or down. He had reached the point of certain failure.

"It's too big for me!"

I rushed over. "Are you okay, son?" I asked from the bottom of the ladder.

He looked down at me, shaken but clinging to that ladder with steely determination. And I could tell he had a question ready.

"Dad, will you come down the slide with me?" he asked. The teenager was losing patience, but I wasn't about to let the moment go.

"Why, son?" I asked, peering up into his little face.

"I can't do it without you, Dad," he said, trembling. "It's too big for me!"

I stretched as high as I could to reach him and lifted him into my arms. Then we climbed that long ladder up to the clouds together. At the top, I put my son between my legs and wrapped my arms around him. Then we went zipping down the slide together, laughing all the way.

our suff

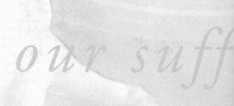

HIS HAND, HIS SPIRIT

That is what your Father's hand is like. You tell Him, "Father, please do this in me because I can't do it alone! It's too big for me!" And you step out in faith to do and say things that could only come from His hand. Afterwards, your spirit is shouting, *God did that, nobody else! God carried me, gave me the words, gave me the power—and it is wonderful!*

I couldn't recommend more highly living in this supernatural dimension!

God's power under us, in us, surging through us is exactly what turns dependence into unforgettable experiences of completeness. "Not that we are sufficient of ourselves," wrote Paul, "to think of anything as being from ourselves, but our sufficiency is from God, who also made us sufficient as ministers of the new covenant" (2 CORINTHIANS 3:5–6).

Tragic as it might sound, the hand of the Lord is so seldom experienced by even mature Christians that they don't miss it and don't ask for it. They hardly know it exists. They think of it as something reserved for prophets and apostles, but not for them. As you'd expect, when these believers arrive at points of certain failure, they tend to come to the wrong conclusion: *I've gone too far; I've ended up in the wrong place. And since I already have all the resources I'm going to get, I need to exit fast!*

Jabez, by contrast, was so certain that God's hand upon him was necessary for blessing that he couldn't imagine a life of honor without it. Let's look more closely at the meaning of his prayer.

The "hand of the Lord" is a biblical term for God's power and presence in the lives of His people (SEE JOSHUA 4:24 AND ISAIAH 59:1). In Acts, the phenomenal success of the early church was attributed to one thing: "The hand of the Lord was with them, and a great number believed and turned to the Lord" (ACTS 11:21). A more specific New Testament description for God's hand is "the filling of the Holy Spirit." The church's growth bears powerful witness to both the necessity and availability of the hand of God to accomplish the business of God.

Consider the natural progression from more blessing to more territory to the need for supernatural power. When Jesus gave His disciples the Great Commission—"Go therefore and make disciples of all the nations…and lo, I am with you always" (MATTHEW 28:19–20)—He was bestowing on them both an incredible blessing and an impossible task. Into all the world and preach? Certainly a disaster in the making! After all, He was commissioning such unreliable cowards as Peter, who had already proved that a girl by a campfire could get him to deny he'd ever heard of Jesus!

Yet when He sent the Holy Spirit (ACTS 1:8), Jesus touched these ordinary believers with greatness, filling them with His miraculous power to spread the Gospel. In fact, you'll notice in Luke's account that the phrase "filled with the Spirit" is often linked to a consequence: They "spoke with boldness" (SEE ACTS 4:13; 5:29; 7:51; 9:27). Only God at work *through them* could account for the miracles and mass conversions that followed.

When we ask for God's mighty presence like Jabez and the early church did, we will also see tremendous results that can be explained only as from the hand of God.

What strikes me about the early church was that believers continually sought to be filled by God (SEE ACTS 4:23–31). They were known as a community who spent hours and even days in prayer together, waiting upon God and asking for His power (SEE ACTS 2:42–47). They were longing to receive more of God's "hand"—a fresh spiritual in-filling of God's power that would turn impending, certain failure into a miracle and make their extraordinary assignment possible.

Paul told the Christians at Ephesus to make it a priority to be "filled with all the fullness of God" (EPHESIANS 3:19). To that end, he prayed that God would bless and strengthen them "with might through His Spirit" (3:16).

When was the last time your church got together and pleaded for the filling of the Spirit? When was the last time you petitioned God regularly and fervently, "Oh, put Your hand upon me! Fill me with Your Spirit!"? The rapid spread of the Good News in the Roman world couldn't have happened any other way.

twelve TEENS AND AN EGG

Many years ago, while I was serving as a youth pastor at a large church in New Jersey, twelve high school kids proved to me that the hand of God is available to every believer who asks. For a summer ministry project we had prayerfully set our sights on suburban Long Island, New York. Objective: to evangelize the youth of the area in six weeks.

We decided on a three-part strategy. We would begin with backyard Bible studies, switch to beach evangelism in the afternoon, and then wrap it up with an evening outreach through local churches. Sounds simple, but I don't have to tell you that the team—youth pastor included—felt overwhelmed by the size of the task.

We invited a specialist in children's ministry on Long Island to give us some training. He told our missionary band that getting thirteen or fourteen kids in a backyard club would be a smashing success. After he left, I quietly said, "If we don't have one hundred kids in each club by the end of the week, we should consider it a failure."

Suddenly, all of us wanted to get down on our knees and pray.

"Lord, please bless us!"

off something

I'll never forget those young, earnest prayers. "Lord, please bless us!" and "Lord, I know it's way over my head, but please, give me a hundred kids!" and "Lord, by Your Spirit, pull off something great for Your glory!"

Parents kept telling our team that what we were attempting was impossible. And I'm sure they were right. But it started happening. Four of the six teams had more than a hundred children crammed into their meetings that first week. Some groups had to move to homes where two backyards adjoined without fences so all the kids could fit. By week's end we had shared the Good News with more than five hundred children, most of whom had never been to church.

If that wasn't enough miracles, the beach phase of our mission to Long Island brought more—helped along by a little magic. Actually, I went into a local novelty shop and came back to the group with a beginner's magic kit. You know, "everything you need to amaze and impress your friends." I stayed up until 3:00 A.M. learning how to make an egg "disappear." By the next afternoon, we were unrolling our free magic show in the sand and pleading with God for His hand to be upon us.

twelve TEENS

Specifically, we were asking the Lord for thirty decisions for salvation *by the end of the first day.*

Our audience grew from a single row of squirming children (dropped off by parents who wanted a few minutes of peace) to more than 150 bathing-suited customers. We rotated the entertainment from magic shows to storytelling to Gospel presentations. Parents began edging closer. Finally clusters of teenagers started swelling our crowd. By the end of the afternoon we had reached a count of 250. And when we finally gave an invitation, no fewer than thirty people indicated they wanted to accept Jesus Christ as their Savior—right there on the beach.

Once we had established our beach ministry, we added evening crusades for youth in local churches. God blessed our efforts beyond anyone's expectation—but right in line with the scope of our Jabez prayer. By the end of our six-week invasion, we could count twelve hundred new believers on Long Island, all of whom received helps and follow-up material.

Those twelve high school kids returned to their comfortable, middle-class lives in the suburbs convinced that *God can do anything.* The first thing that changed was their home church because they decided to pray for the Holy Spirit to move in their own congregation and bring repentance and revival.

Impossible? Not at all. Twelve kids and a youth sponsor watched as God's hand moved through the church. As the members of the mission team shared their stories and challenged the church to ask God for more, revival swept through that church like no one could remember.

All because twelve students asked for blessings indeed, for more territory for God's glory, and for His hand of power to be upon them.

father's TOUCH

A FATHER'S TOUCH

Like any loving dad at the playground, God is watching and waiting for you to ask for the supernatural power He offers. "For the eyes of the Lord run to and fro throughout the whole earth, to show Himself strong on behalf of those whose heart is loyal to Him" (2 CHRONICLES 16:9). Notice that our God is not scanning the horizon for spiritual giants or seminary standouts. He eagerly seeks those who are sincerely loyal to Him. Your loyal heart is the only part of His expansion plan that He will not provide.

You and I are always only one plea away from inexplicable, Spirit-enabled exploits. By His touch you can experience supernatural enthusiasm, boldness, and power. It's up to you.

Ask every day for the Father's touch.

Because for the Christian, *dependence* is just another word for power.

dependence
another word for power

KEEPING THE
LEGACY SAFE

Oh, that You would keep me from evil!

A full-page magazine ad depicts a Roman gladiator in big trouble. Somehow, he has dropped his sword. The enraged lion, seeing its opportunity, is in mid-lunge, jaws wide. The crowd in the Colosseum is on its feet, watching in horror as the panic-stricken gladiator tries to flee. The caption reads: Sometimes you can afford to come in second. Sometimes you can't.

After asking for and receiving supernatural blessing, influence, and power, Jabez might have believed that he could jump into any ring with any lion—and win. You would think that a person with the hand of God upon him would pray, "Keep me through evil."

But Jabez understood what that doomed gladiator didn't: By far our most important strategy for defeating the roaring lion is to stay out of the arena. That's why the final request of his prayer was that God would keep him out of the fight:

"Oh…keep me from evil."

THE LEGACY

Jabez's last request is a brilliant but little-understood strategy for sustaining a blessed life. After all, as your life transcends the ordinary and starts to encroach on new territory for God, guess whose turf you're invading?

In the previous chapter our prayer was for supernatural power to work through our weakness; in this one our petition is for supernatural help to protect us from Satan's proven ability to make us come in second.

THE PERILS OF SPIRITUAL SUCCESS

Without doubt, success brings with it greater opportunities for failure. Just look around at the Christian leaders who have fallen into sin, dropped out of ministry, and left in their wake untold numbers of shaken, disillusioned, and injured people. As someone once said, blessedness is the greatest of perils because "it tends to dull our keen sense of dependence on God and make us prone to presumption."

The further along in a life of supernatural service you get, the more you'll need the final plea of Jabez's prayer. You are going to experience more attacks on you and your family. You are going to become familiar with the enemy's unwelcome barbs—distraction, opposition, and oppression, for starters. In fact, if your experience is anything *but* that, be concerned.

I'll never forget overhearing a conversation in seminary between a fellow student and my mentor, Professor Howard Hendricks. The student was excited to tell Dr. Hendricks how well his life was going.

"When I first came here," he said, "I was so tempted and tested I could barely keep my head above water. But now—praise God!—my life at seminary has smoothed out. I'm not being tempted hardly at all!"

But Hendricks looked deeply alarmed—not the reaction the student was expecting. "That's about the worst thing I could have heard," he told the surprised senior. "That shows me that you're no longer in the battle! Satan isn't worried about you anymore."

We were redeemed and commissioned for the front lines. That's why praying to be kept from evil is such a vital part of the blessed life.

Along with many others, I've discovered that the one time I'm particularly in need of this part of Jabez's prayer is when I have just experienced a spiritual success. Paradoxically, that's when I'm most inclined to hold a wrong (and dangerous) view of my strengths.

Years ago, a cab had picked me up in downtown Chicago and was whisking me down the Kennedy Expressway toward the airport. I slumped in the backseat, exhausted from a week of special meetings at Moody Bible Institute. God had moved in remarkable ways. I had preached every day and counseled scores of students—seventy-six, to be exact (I kept a log). Now heading home, I was physically and spiritually spent. Staring blankly out at the traffic, I reached for the Jabez prayer.

"O Lord," I pleaded, *"I have no resistance left. I'm completely worn out in Your service. I can't cope with temptation. Please, keep evil far from me today."*

When I boarded the plane, I found I'd been assigned a middle seat—not a good start for my flight. And things quickly got worse. The man on my left pulled out a pornographic magazine. *"Lord, I thought we had a deal here!"* I groaned in my spirit, and I looked the other way. But before the plane lifted off, the man on my right opened his briefcase and pulled out his own skin magazine.

At that moment, I didn't have it in me to ask them to change their reading material. I closed my eyes. *"Lord,"* I prayed, *"I can't cope with this today. Please chase evil far away!"*

Suddenly the man on my right swore, folded up his magazine, and put it away. I looked at him to see what had prompted his action. Nothing, as far as I could tell. Then the man on the left looked at him, swore loudly, and closed up his magazine, too. Again, I could find no apparent reason for his decision.

We were over Indiana when I began laughing uncontrollably. They both asked me what was so funny.

"Gentlemen," I said, "you wouldn't believe me if I told you!"

playing KEEP AWAY

PLAYING KEEP AWAY

We've arrived at one of Satan's hidden strongholds in believers' lives. In my experience, most Christians seem to pray solely for strength to endure temptations—for victory over the attacks of our raging adversary, Satan.

Somehow we don't think to ask God simply to keep us away from temptation and keep the devil at bay in our lives.

But in the model prayer Jesus gave His followers, nearly a quarter of its fifty words ask for deliverance: "And do not lead us into temptation, but deliver us from the evil one" (MATTHEW 6:13). Nothing about spiritual insight or special powers. Not a word about confrontation.

When was the last time you asked God to keep you away from temptation? In the same way that God wants you to ask for more blessing, more territory, and more power, He longs to hear you plead for safekeeping from evil.

Without a temptation, we would not sin. Most of us face too many temptations—and therefore sin too often—because we don't ask God to lead us away from temptation. We make a huge spiritual leap forward, therefore, when we begin to focus less on beating temptation and more on avoiding it.

With all the legions of heaven at His disposal, even Jesus prayed for deliverance. Even with all His divine insight, when He was tempted in the wilderness, He refused to engage Satan in a discussion about his enticing offers.

As we move deeper into the realm of the miraculous, the most effective war against sin that we can wage is to pray that we will not have to fight unnecessary temptation. And God offers us His supernatural power to do just that.

deliver us from the evil one

DROPPING OUR WEAPONS

DROPPING OUR WEAPONS

The arena of temptation is usually enemy territory. By this, I don't mean that being tempted is the same thing as sinning—that's another of Satan's deceptions. What I mean is that we're usually asked to duke it out with evil in the spheres of our subjective experience. This isn't neutral ground, because we're fallen creatures with limited understandings, as Satan well knows. Here, even our finest weapons (humanly speaking) can quickly become our undoing.

Take our wisdom. It works sporadically at best because the nature of evil is to deceive us with a little bit of the truth—not all of it, mind you, but just enough to trick us. Adam and Eve weren't any more prone to succumb to temptation than we are. In fact, unlike us, they were perfect in every way, and none of their genuine needs were unmet. Satan approached the human race at its peak of promise and performance—and crushed us with one friendly conversation.

That's why, like Jabez, we should pray for protection from deception:

> *Lord, keep me from making the mistakes I'm most prone to when temptation comes.*
> *I confess that what I think is necessary, smart, or personally beneficial is so often*
> *only the beautiful wrapping on sin. So please, keep evil far from me!*

Take our experience. The further we move into new territory for Christ, the less protected are our flanks from Satan's attacks. Someone has said, "Your danger is not in being on the edge of a precipice, but in being unwatchful there." A tiny indulgence of pride or self-confidence can spell disaster. The deepest grief I've seen in fellow believers is among those who have experienced extraordinary blessings, territory, and power...only to slip into serious sin.

Like Jabez, then, we should ask to be spared dangerous misjudgments:

> *Lord, keep me safe from the pain and grief that sin brings.*
> *For the dangers that I can't see, or the ones that I think I can*
> *risk because of my experience (pride and carelessness), put up*
> *a supernatural barrier. Protect me, Father, by your power!*

Take our feelings. Do we really understand how far the American Dream is from God's dream for us? We're steeped in a culture that worships freedom, independence, personal rights, and the pursuit of pleasure. We respect people who sacrifice to get what they want. But to be a living sacrifice? To be crucified to self?

Like Jabez, we should plead to be kept from the powerful pull of what feels right to us but is wrong:

> *Lord, keep me safe from temptations that pull at my emotions and*
> *my physical needs, that call out to my sense of what I deserve, what*
> *I have the "right" to feel and enjoy. Because You are the true source of*
> *all that is really life, direct my steps away from all that is not of You.*

These are petitions for deliverance that our Father loves to hear—and answer.

witness to FREEDOM

WITNESS TO FREEDOM

Since Satan most opposes those who are becoming the greatest threat to him and his kingdom, the more God answers your Jabez prayers, the more you should be prepared to confront spiritual attack.

Sometimes, however, you cannot be kept from evil because by God's power you are attempting to launch a D-Day offensive against the darkness. At those times you can stand confidently against the enemy with what Paul calls "the weapons of our warfare" (2 CORINTHIANS 10:4).

I remember a prayer meeting in the early years of the Promise Keepers movement. The twenty-five members of our leadership team for the event were huddled in prayer as tens of thousands gathered in the stadium below. The opposition was so thick that we kept stumbling over our words and falling silent. Unless we could defeat Satan's oppression, we knew there would be no point in starting the program. Finally one of the team members stood up and began to attack evil with the truth.

"Friends, the victory is already ours," he declared confidently while we continued to kneel. Utterly determined, he began praying the truth of God's will for that day back to God. His memorable prayer went something like this:

> *Lord, it is Your will that we seek this blessing for countless men and their families! We know that it is Your deepest desire to take more ground for the kingdom in this generation, on this day in history, in this stadium! And we thank You for what You're going to do.*

The best the rest of us could do at first was to labor along with him in prayer, casting ourselves upon the Lord to move in us and on our behalf. The heaviness we felt was almost too much to bear. But our prayer leader didn't falter:

> *Father, it is Your profound and immovable purpose that Your Holy Spirit be here—is here now in our midst—moving already through the rows of gathering men. You have come here to work in a supernatural dimension that even we can barely comprehend, but which we earnestly anticipate. And at Your name, Lord Jesus, every other power on earth must bow or flee.*

At some point in his prayer, we broke through with God. Our desperate pleas turned to praise and worship. We knew we had been witnesses to freedom in the Spirit. We strode together out into that arena to boldly claim the bountiful results of what had already been accomplished in prayer.

legacy OF TRIUMPH

A LEGACY OF TRIUMPH

I think Jabez would have liked that prayer. He wanted to live free from the bondage of evil because God's trustworthy character and steadfast Word had shown him something unimaginably better.

"Stay out of the arena of temptation whenever possible," he would advise, "but never live in fear or defeat. By God's power, you can keep your legacy of blessing safe."

Do you believe that a supernatural God is going to show up to keep you from evil and protect your spiritual investment? Jabez did believe, and he acted on his belief. Thereafter his life was spared from the grief and pain that evil brings.

Paul told the Colossians that God had made them "alive together with [Christ]" and that having "disarmed principalities and powers, He made a public spectacle of them, triumphing over them in [the cross]" (COLOSSIANS 2:13, 15).

KEEPING

LEGACY SAFE

What an amazing declaration of victory! Through Christ, we can live in triumph—not in temptation or defeat. With the fourth plea of Jabez as part of our life, we are now ready to move up to a higher level of honor and exponentially expanding blessings.

Here's why: Unlike in most stock portfolios, in God's kingdom the safest investment also shows the most remarkable growth.

God made you alive with Christ

ALIVE by the cross

WELCOME

TO GOD'S HONOR

Jabez was more honorable than his brothers.

ROLL

Do you think God has favorites? Certainly God makes His love available to all, and Jesus came to earth so that "whosoever" might call on His name and be saved.

But Jabez, whose prayer earned him a "more honorable" award from God, might have made the case that God does have favorites. His experience taught him that equal access to God's favor does not add up to equal reward. What happened to some of the others named along with him in Chronicles? Idbash, Hazelelponi, and Anub, for example. What honors and awards did they get from God?

Simply put, God favors those who ask. He holds back nothing from those who want and earnestly long for what He wants.

a life marked
by God's blessings

To say that you want to be "more honorable" in God's eyes is not arrogance or self-centeredness. "More honorable" describes what God thinks; it's not credit we take for ourselves. You would be giving in to a carnal impulse if you were trying to outdo someone else, but you are living in the Spirit when you strive to receive God's highest reward. "I press toward the goal for the prize," Paul wrote in his last epistle (PHILIPPIANS 3:14), and he looked forward to the day he could give an account for what he had done (2 CORINTHIANS 5:9–10).

The sorrowful alternative does not appeal to me. I don't want to get to heaven and hear God say: "Let's look at your life, Bruce. Let me show you what I wanted for you and tried repeatedly to accomplish through you…but you wouldn't let me." What a travesty!

I've noticed that winning honor nearly always means leaving mediocre expectations and comfortable assumptions behind. But in this case it has very little to do with talent. How encouraging it is to find very few supersaints listed among those God has placed on His honor roll (HEBREWS 11). They are mostly ordinary, easy-to-overlook people who had faith in an extraordinary, miraculous God and stepped out to act on that faith.

What they discovered was a life marked by God's blessings, supernatural provision, and divine leading *at the very moment they needed them.*

God's HAND ON ME

I think the immediacy—the "now-ness"—of serving God is one of the most exciting aspects of living for God's honor roll. You start to thrive in the present to a degree most Christians have never thought possible.

Think about it: How would your day unfold if you believed that God wants your borders expanded at all times with every person and if you were confident that God's powerful hand is directing you even as you minister?

During the past five years, I've been putting that belief to a very specific test, often with astounding results. I ask the Lord for more ministry; then, following the nudging of the Holy Spirit, I initiate a conversation with a person by asking a simple question: "How can I help you?"

Let me give you an example:

I was driving through Atlanta to the airport on my way to an important speaking engagement in North Carolina. Without warning, traffic slowed, then stopped. A major accident had blocked all lanes. When it became clear that I was going to miss my flight, I prayed, "Lord, please make my flight late so I can catch it."

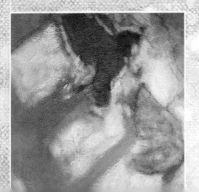

When I finally arrived at the concourse for departure, I noticed scores of people milling around. Sure enough, the flight had been delayed. Humbled and thankful, I found myself wondering if God had something else in mind as well. I began to pray that the Lord would arrange an appointment for ministry.

Within moments, a well-dressed businesswoman approached, pulling her leather roller bag. When she joined the rest of us to wait for the flight, I noticed she seemed flustered.

I nodded hello, then asked, "What can I do for you?"

"What?" she said, not quite believing her ears.

I repeated my offer.

"You can't do anything for me," she said, kindly but firmly.

"Well, I believe there's something I can do for you, but I don't know what it is. But you do. My name is Bruce, by the way." Then I smiled at her and calmly asked again, "So, what can I do for you?"

Jabez

Friend, have you ever seen the Holy Spirit break through emotional and spiritual barriers right before your eyes? It's an experience you won't forget. The woman caught her breath, leaned against the wall, and started to talk. "Well, I'm flying home to divorce my husband," she said. "That's why I'm waiting to catch this flight."

Tears welled up in her eyes. I suggested we move to a quieter corner in the departure area, and I asked the Lord to place His protection around us and between us.

Her name was Sophie. Her perfectly tailored dress and Italian leather accessories hid a broken person on the run from disappointment and despair. Her husband had been unfaithful to her and hurt her in other ways. Even though he wanted to make things right, she had had enough. When she got home, she would be pulling divorce papers out of her briefcase.

The gate attendant interrupted us. "Asheville, right? You're going to miss your plane." We were the last two to board. Now Sophie was agitated because our conversation would have to end, and she wasn't finished.

was more honorable...

"The Lord will put us together," I said, not quite believing the confidence I heard in my voice.

"What do you mean?" Sophie asked.

"Well, He didn't have too much difficulty making the earth; He can get us two seats together."

But when we compared tickets, we were five rows apart. As we arrived at my seat, the man sitting in the middle seat next to Sophie heard us talking and turned around. "I hate middle seats," he said. "I'll switch so you can sit together."

Sophie sank into the seat beside me, momentarily speechless. During the flight, we talked about her options. I laid out some biblical principles and promises for her. I prayed with her. And by the time we landed in Asheville, she had broken through to forgiveness. She was still hurting, but she was at peace, determined to give her marriage the commitment it deserved.

expec

As I look back over this divine appointment, I can see the footprints of Jabez and his little prayer:

- I asked for and expected God's blessing *for today.*

- I pleaded for more "territory" (more ministry and influence for Him) and stepped forward to receive it.

- I leaned precariously but confidently upon the Holy Spirit to guide my thoughts, words, and actions with Sophie and to work in the supernatural realm to accomplish what I could not.

- I asked God to keep evil (or in this case, even a hint of impropriety) from spoiling the blessing He desired to bring about through me.

Let me encourage you, friend, to reach boldly for the miracle. Your Father knows your gifts, your hindrances, and the condition you're in at every moment. And He also knows something you can't possibly know—every single person who's in desperate need of receiving His touch through you. God will bring you to that person at exactly the right time and in the right circumstances.

And at that moment, you will receive power to be His witness.

God's blessing today

cycle OF BLESSINGS

THE CYCLE OF BLESSINGS

As you repeat the steps, you will set in motion a cycle of blessing that will keep multiplying what God is able to do in and through you. This is the exponential growth I referred to at the close of the previous chapter. You have asked for and received more blessing, more territory, more power, and more protection. But the growth curve soon starts to spike upwards.

You don't reach the next level of blessing and stay there. You begin again—*Lord, bless me indeed! Lord, please enlarge…!* And so on. As the cycle repeats itself, you'll find that you are steadily moving into wider spheres of blessing and influence, spiraling ever outward and upward into a larger life for God.

The day will come—and come repeatedly during your life—that you will be so overwhelmed with God's graciousness that tears will stream down your face. I can remember saying to the Lord, "It's too much! Hold some of your blessings back!" If you're like many who use the Jabez prayer, including me, you'll come to times in your life when you feel so blessed that you stop praying for more, at least for a while.

But I promise you that you will see a direct link: You will know beyond doubt that God has opened heaven's storehouses *because you prayed.*

I'll admit: The cycle of blessings will give your faith a good testing. Will you let God work in your life regardless of what He chooses? It will always be for your best. Will you surrender to His power and love and surprising plan for you? I hope you choose to do just that. You will experience the joy of knowing that God experiences deep pleasure and joy in *you!*

The only thing that can break this cycle of abundant living is sin, because sin breaks the flow of God's power. It is as if the electric lines to your house in Phoenix were severed and you were cut off from the immense power generators at Hoover Dam. All the incredible potential of the dam's turbines would be untapped, wasted, and waiting for the connection to be restored.

You should know that when you sin after experiencing the Jabez blessing, you'll experience a deeper grief over your disconnect from God than you ever thought possible. It's the pain that comes from having once tasted the exhilaration of God working in you at a higher level of fulfillment and then turning back.

I encourage you to rush back into God's presence and make things right, whatever it takes. Don't squander even for a minute the miracle that He has started in your life. Indescribable good still lies ahead for you and your family.

MAKING
JABEZ MINE

So God granted him what he requested.

I challenge you to make the Jabez prayer for blessing part of the daily fabric of your life. To do that, I encourage you to follow unwaveringly the plan outlined here for the next thirty days. By the end of that time, you'll be noticing significant changes in your life, and the prayer will be on its way to becoming a treasured, lifelong habit.

1. Pray the Jabez prayer every morning, and keep a record of your daily prayer by marking off a calendar or a chart you make especially for the purpose.

2. Write out the prayer and tape it in your Bible, in your day-timer, on your bathroom mirror, or some other place where you'll be reminded of your new vision.

3. Reread this little book once each week during the next month, asking God to show you important insights you may have missed.

4. Tell one other person of your commitment to your new prayer habit, and ask him or her to check up on you.

5. Begin to keep a record of changes in your life, especially the divine appointments and new opportunities you can relate directly to the Jabez prayer.

6. Start praying the Jabez prayer for your family, friends, and local church.

Of course, what you *know about* this or any other prayer won't get you anything. What you know about deliverance won't deliver you from anything. You can hang the Jabez prayer on the wall of every room in your house and nothing will happen. It's only what you believe will happen *and therefore do next* that will release God's power for you and bring about a life change. But when you act, you will step up to God's best for you.

I'm living proof.

making Jabez mine

the rest OF THE STORY

In the first chapter of this book, I told you how choosing to pray for a larger work for God redirected the course and quality of my life. Let me tell you the rest of the story.

My wife and I took our first step to making the Jabez prayer a regular part of our spiritual journey in that yellow kitchen in Dallas with a Texas rainstorm rattling the windows. We wanted so much to reach for more—to do and become all that God had in mind for us. But we had no idea what would happen.

Over the years at Walk Thru the Bible, our once feeble prayers have grown because *He has never stopped answering!* I can remember when we had twenty-five or thirty Bible conferences in a year. This year Walk Thru will conduct over twenty-five hundred Bible conferences— fifty each weekend. The ministry now publishes ten magazines each month to help individuals and families grow in God's Word every day. We recently passed the 100 million mark in total issues published.

I don't mention these numbers to impress you. I share this story because it is a very personal one and, to me at least, almost shocking evidence of what God's grace and Jabez praying can do.

Now God has stretched our faith yet again. Recently we found ourselves asking an entirely different question—not so much "Lord, enlarge our borders" as "Lord, what are *Your* borders? What do *You* want done?"

Obviously, His borders encompass the whole world. Clearly, it is His complete will for us to reach the world—*right now!* So our leadership team began to ask how we could be part of making that happen. Soon we decided to pray the biggest little prayer we could imagine: *O God—let us reach the whole world for You.*

In January 1998 we began WorldTeach, birthed from the womb of the Jabez prayer. WorldTeach is an exciting fifteen-year vision to establish the largest Bible-teaching faculty in the world—120,000—a Bible teacher for every 50,000 people on earth. As I write this closing section, I'm in India to help train Bible teachers from six nations to take the Great Commission into every village and city and nation.

Just by looking at what is happening, I can assure you that God still answers those who have a loyal heart and pray the Jabez prayer. By its second year, WorldTeach had launched in twenty-three nations—including Russia, India, South Africa, Ukraine, and Singapore—and enrolled twenty-five hundred teachers. Our target for our third year is thirty-five nations and five thousand teachers. And we are running ahead of schedule.

One national missions leader told me that WorldTeach has had the fastest launch of any Christian ministry in history. Humanly speaking, this kind of growth is unexplainable. We are only weak humans who seek to be clean and fully surrendered to our Lord, to want what He wants for His world, and to step forward in His power and protection to see it happen now.

I don't know what you call that, but I have always called it the miracle of Jabez.

God never stops answering!

redeemed

FOR THIS

REDEEMED FOR THIS

I've seen something amazing happen in people like you who have suspected all along that God answers courageous prayers. When the merest ray of faith shines in your spirit, the warmth of God's truth infuses you, and you instinctively want to cry out, "Oh, Lord, please…bless me!" And I see in people like you a growing excitement and an anticipation of what will happen next.

Because something always does. Your spiritual expectations undergo a radical shift, though it might be only slightly apparent to someone else. You feel renewed confidence in the present-tense power and reality of your prayers because you know you're praying in the will and pleasure of God. You sense in the deepest recesses of your being the rightness of praying like this. You know beyond a doubt that you were redeemed for this: to ask Him for the God-sized best He has in mind for you, and to ask for it with all your heart.

Join me for that transformation. You will change your legacy and bring supernatural blessings wherever you go. God will release His miraculous power in your life now. And for all eternity, He will lavish on you His honor and delight.

we were redeemed for this

And Jabez called on the God of Israel saying,

"Oh, that You would bless me indeed,

and enlarge my territory,

that Your hand would be with me

and that You would keep me from evil,

that I may not cause pain!"

So God granted him what he requested.